What's My Time Style?

We all have our own style of managing time. We express that style in everything we do at work — whether it's beginning a new project, handling an interruption, managing multiple tasks, arranging our workspace, participating in a meeting, or sharing a task with a coworker. To make your individual time style work to your best advantage, you first need to identify it.

Directions

For each statement below, choose the statement ending that most closely reflects the way you manage time. Sometimes you will find that more than one statement describes you. In that case, choose the one that most closely represents your style of managing time. Circle the letter you have chosen on the Response Form.

1. When I begin a project, the first thing I do is …
   a. Collect all the data that I'll need.
   b. Bounce ideas off other people.
   c. Seek input from everyone.
   d. Jump right in.

2. I approach paperwork by …
   a. Beginning with the items people have asked me for.
   b. Sifting and sorting it, item by item.
   c. Attacking top priority items.
   d. Beginning with the items that look most energizing.

3. Once I have handed over work to someone else, I …

    a. Often step back in to solve problems.

    b. Occasionally ask the other person how it's going.

    c. Supply lots of positive feedback.

    d. Ask detailed questions about how the person is performing the work.

4. When someone asks me to take on another project and my plate is already full, I …

    a. Accept the new project but worry that I may not be able to take care of everyone's needs.

    b. Say "no" unless I view the new project as urgent.

    c. Make room for the new project if it seems more interesting.

    d. Evaluate where to place the new project in my work lineup.

5. When a project is stalled because people can't agree on which action to take, I …

    a. Analyze the different positions to see which one makes most sense.

    b. Work to bring people together.

    c. Forge ahead, even if it means placing limits on input from others.

    d. Try to re-energize people.

6. The first thing I do when I arrive at work is …

    a. Hope that something unexpected will occur to change the week's routine.

    b. Check in with coworkers to see how they're doing.

    c. Start organizing my work using a paper or electronic planner.

    d. Get down to the most important business and tune out the noise around me.

7. I like to organize my papers by …

    a. Tossing papers into loose piles.

    b. Filing them in the appropriate folders.

    c. Keeping items related to current projects within quick reach.

    d. Using a system that I think others can easily understand in case they need access to my papers.

8. When someone offers to help me with a project, I …

    a. Am hesitant. I think about whether helping me would place too much of a burden on the other person.

    b. Am eager. "Two heads are better than one."

    c. Am reluctant. The other person may not analyze the information accurately.

    d. Turn the person down. I can't count on other people to move as quickly as I do.

Response Form

Directions: Circle the letter that corresponds to the statement ending that most clearly reflects the way you manage time. Work your way *down* each column. The items are numbered consecutively by columns, not rows.

1	8	15
a	a	a
b	b	b
c	c	c
d	d	d

2	9	16
a	a	a
b	b	b
c	c	c
d	d	d

3	10	17
a	a	a
b	b	b
c	c	c
d	d	d

4	11	18
a	a	a
b	b	b
c	c	c
d	d	d

5	12	19
a	a	a
b	b	b
c	c	c
d	d	d

6	13	20
a	a	a
b	b	b
c	c	c
d	d	d

7	14	21
a	a	a
b	b	b
c	c	c
d	d	d

Demographics

Industry: _____

Title: _____

Gender: M   F

Age: 18-35   36-50   51+

What's My Time Style?

9. Small talk at the beginning of meetings makes me feel …
   a. Uncomfortable. I'd rather not get into personal topics.
   b. Impatient. We need to get moving.
   c. Energized. I can tell there'll be some good give-and-take.
   d. Comfortable. We can all get to know one another so we can work better together.

10. When I'm given some lead-time on a project, I …
    a. Evaluate how best to budget my time.
    b. Wait until the last minute. I work best under pressure.
    c. Plunge right in. I can't relax until it's done.
    d. Consider where the project fits into my commitments to other people.

11. Within view of my desk, I like to keep …
    a. A list of major milestones I need to reach.
    b. A detailed schedule related to current projects.
    c. Motivational sayings to keep me focused.
    d. Pictures of loved ones to brighten my day.

12. When my group arrives at a decision quickly, I feel …
    a. Dissatisfied. We may have oversimplified the situation.
    b. Concerned. We may have overlooked other people's opinions.
    c. Relieved. Now we can move on to the next item.
    d. Disappointed. We may have closed off some creative discussion.

13. When I'm busy and someone stops by "just to say 'hi,'" I usually …
    a. Become impatient to get back to the project I'm working on.
    b. Feel distracted from the details I've been focusing on.
    c. Take the opportunity to see how the person is doing.
    d. Am relieved to have some variety in my day.

14. In making decisions, I like to …
    a. Make everyone feel included.
    b. Cut to the chase.
    c. Gather and evaluate all the data before acting.
    d. Toss around fresh, new ideas with people in my group.

15. When my workspace becomes cluttered, I …
    a. Become merciless. "When in doubt, throw it out."
    b. Put all the old papers in a file because someone may need them later.
    c. Get creative. I toss related items into loose piles or folders.
    d. Start organizing. "A place for everything, everything in its place."

16. When I'm faced with multiple requests for my time, I …

    a. Jump into the task that looks most fun.

    b. Set priorities by carefully reviewing my group's overall goals.

    c. Delve into the task that I view as most pressing.

    d. Pause to think about who will benefit the most from my help.

17. If I'm in charge of keeping time at a meeting, I …

    a. Feel pleased if everyone has had time to contribute.

    b. Make sure we cover each agenda item thoroughly.

    c. Place limits on people's input so that we can wrap up on time.

    d. Find that we've gone over time because of all the give-and-take.

18. When I'm in the middle of an important project and the phone rings, I …

    a. Pick it up hoping for a social break.

    b. Ignore it. It's more important to push the project over the finish line.

    c. Answer it. I think of how the caller would feel if I didn't pick it up.

    d. Let my voice mail pick it up. Later I return messages in order of priority.

19. I am most comfortable in discussions when …

    a. People get to the point immediately.

    b. The group takes the time to hear each person's opinion.

    c. The group walks through points one by one.

    d. People produce ideas on the spur of the moment.

20. My workspace …

    a. Looks messy, but I have a knack for finding what I want.

    b. Looks comfortable. I want visitors to feel welcome.

    c. Is carefully organized with every item in the right place.

    d. Has lots of space for me to spread out my work.

21. When I'm at a brainstorming session, I …

    a. Think the exchange of ideas is fun.

    b. Feel reassured when I know that everyone is being included.

    c. Find many of the ideas people offer to be random and imprecise.

    d. Feel as though people are going in circles and getting nowhere fast.

Scoring *What's My Time Style?*

What's My Time Style? can be scored quickly and easily by following these steps:

Step 1   Begin by separating the Response Form from the Scoring Form and Data Collection Form by slipping a pencil or finger between the first and second pages and gently separating them. Or separate them at the inside perforation.

Step 2   Now follow the directions on the Scoring Form. Count the number of times you circled each style and place the resulting totals in the corresponding Style Total shapes.

Step 3   Copy the Style Totals into the corresponding squares of Chart 1: My Time Style Profile.

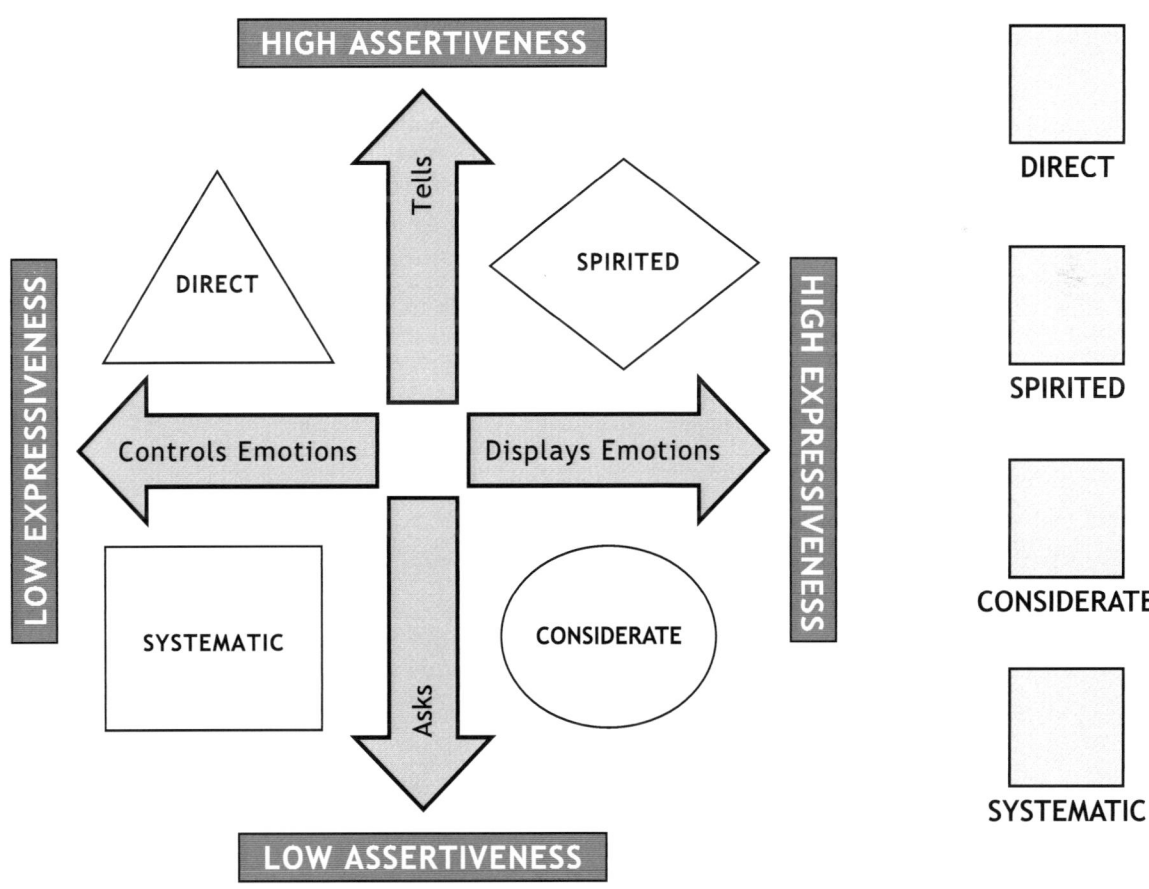

CHART 1: My Time Style Profile

What is Time Style?

Each of the four time styles is based on the degree of assertiveness and expressiveness exhibited. The four styles are:

Direct = *High assertiveness, low expressiveness*

Spirited = *High assertiveness, high expressiveness*

Considerate = *Low assertiveness, high expressiveness*

Systematic = *Low assertiveness, low expressiveness*

Your time style comes through whether or not you are aware of it. The style that you use most often is called your dominant style. If you look at your time style profile in Chart 1 on page 5, you can see whether you have one dominant style. A dominant style would be indicated by a score of 8 or above. On the other hand, if you scored 3 or below on any one style, you probably do not use that time management style very often. Although many people have a clearly dominant style, others can manage their time more comfortably using several styles. If you have a relatively even distribution of points, you probably use several styles of time management. You may also use different styles in different situations.

What do you picture yourself doing when you think about managing your time? Many people picture themselves using paper or electronic planners. They may imagine themselves listing their goals and priorities. They may think of the way they've set up their workspace. All these activities are, in fact, important aspects of time management. And they are all personal activities — activities that we perform on our own.

But who among us works in a vacuum? Our workdays are filled with interpersonal situations. A coworker stops by to chat while you're working on a project. A supervisor asks you to take on yet another assignment. You need to hand over work to someone in your group for completion.

In addition to these one-on-one interactions, think of all the group interactions that fill your days. You gather with coworkers informally in the break room, or you attend scheduled meetings. Being productive at work does not simply mean managing your personal time well. It also means managing these one-on-one and group interactions effectively.

The items in *What's My Time Style?* measure both the personal and the interpersonal behaviors we exhibit as we get our jobs done. The following table shows the time management behaviors that are likely to be exhibited by each of the four styles in personal activities, as well as in one-on-one and group interactions.

Your Time Style

We all want to feel that the time we spend at work is time well spent. We want to know that we're productive, and we want to find our work fulfilling. In other words, we all seek to manage our time well. But how we do so varies from person to person. These differences show up in everything we do.

For example, you may like to work through a project step by step and on your own. A coworker down the hall may prefer to bounce ideas off other people and wait until the last minute to complete a project. Yet, one way or another, you are both productive. It's just that you have different approaches to time management.

Your style of managing time (for that matter, your style of performing any activity) is determined by your behavioral style. Think of it as though you have some internal wiring that determines a single style that applies to all your behaviors. For example, you may have noticed that a person whose speech and body language are slow and controlled will typically move through work tasks slowly and systematically. But a person whose speech and body language are fast and uninhibited will usually move through tasks in a faster, less disciplined style. In other words, a specific style colors all of a person's behavior — whether these behaviors involve time management, communication, or any other activity.

The secret of effective time management is to understand your own style of managing time so that you can complete your work easily, in a manner that feels comfortable and natural to you. *What's My Time Style?* will identify your style and familiarize you with the strengths and weaknesses of that style. As a result, you will be able to make your style work for you rather than against you. And by learning about other time styles, you will be able to interact effectively with coworkers who manage their time differently than you.

What's My Time Style? looks at time style in terms of two dimensions: *assertiveness* and *expressiveness*. Assertiveness describes the degree to which a person's behavior is forceful or direct. Expressiveness describes the degree to which a person's behavior is emotionally responsive and open.

The more assertive a person is, the more that person likes to move at a fast pace. In terms of time management, this means that if you are very assertive, you may like to complete tasks quickly — you may direct all your energy toward achieving goals. Or you may enjoy quick, lively interactions with other people — consequently, you're probably successful in moving work forward by motivating others.

The more expressive a person is, the less that person feels the need to control his or her emotions and time. If you're an expressive person, you may like to "wing it" rather than plan your time. Or you may free up a lot of your time to take care of other people's needs. Combine the two dimensions — assertiveness and expressiveness — and the result is four different time styles. To learn about your time style, begin by scoring this instrument using the directions that follow in the next section.

Identifying Different Time Styles

	DIRECT △	SPIRITED ◇	CONSIDERATE ○	SYSTEMATIC □
Personal	■ Directs attention toward reaching goals rather than on the means of reaching them. ■ Makes quick decisions. ■ Has immediate access to needed items. ■ Completes projects by keeping the goal in view.	■ Prefers spontaneity to planning. ■ Doesn't like to close out options. ■ Organizes materials loosely using visual cues. ■ Completes projects by thinking of creative new angles.	■ Focuses on taking care of others' needs. ■ Makes decisions by evaluating others' needs. ■ Keeps items of personal significance within view. ■ Completes projects by thinking of others' needs.	■ Focuses as much on procedure as on final product. ■ Evaluates data before deciding. ■ Keeps every item in its proper place. ■ Completes projects by following procedures.
One-on-One	■ Gets to the point quickly. ■ Focuses on completing tasks rather than on personal information. ■ Likes to retain control when handing over a project. ■ Helps others complete projects by reminding them of the goal and the deadline.	■ Spends more time talking than listening. ■ Prefers to exchange ideas rather than to arrive at conclusions. ■ When handing over work, asks for informal, oral feedback. ■ Helps others complete projects by inspiring them.	■ Listens attentively. ■ Focuses on the other person's needs and methods of handling tasks. ■ When handing over work, provides lots of positive feedback. ■ Helps others complete projects by taking care of their needs, following their methods.	■ Keeps discussion on task-related details. ■ Avoids personal exchanges. ■ When handing over work, provides precise instructions. ■ Helps others complete projects by instructing them in procedure, reminding them of details.
Group	■ Places limits on group discussion. ■ Likes to direct group toward task completion. ■ Speeds up group process by keeping everyone focused on goal.	■ Prefers not to close off discussion. ■ Prefers spontaneous interaction to planning. ■ Speeds up group process by motivating and persuading.	■ Ensures that all members feel valued. ■ Seeks input from everyone. ■ Speeds up group process by making everyone feel valued.	■ Likes to follow an agenda. ■ Prefers to cover every item sequentially. ■ Speeds up group process by confining discussion to the agenda.

TABLE 1: Time Management Behaviors in Personal, One-on-One, and Group Interactions

Time Style Strengths

Each of the four time styles has its own characteristics. Find your dominant style(s) in Chart 2: Time Style Strengths. Put a check mark by the characteristics that best describe your strengths.

Direct

△ Accomplishes tasks quickly

△ Remains on course

△ Makes quick decisions

△ Has immediate access to needed items

Spirited

◇ Thinks of new ways of doing things

◇ Inspires and motivates the group to move the project along

◇ Finds it easy to begin new projects

◇ Handles multiple tasks easily

Systematic

☐ Sets aside time to do the job right

☐ Takes time to analyze and evaluate

☐ Follows procedure carefully

☐ Is thorough with detail

Considerate

○ Devotes time to helping others

○ Adapts easily to others' ways of handling tasks

○ Includes everyone's opinions

○ Moves projects along through active listening

CHART 2: Time Style Strengths

Time Style Trouble Spots

As you can see from Chart 2, each style has definite strengths. However, a style taken to an extreme can become counterproductive. Each style also has weak points. Recognizing your trouble spots is the first step to overcoming them. Chart 3 shows some of the extremes for each style. As you read through them, do you recognize some of your own weak points? Put a check mark by the trouble spots that you have.

Direct

Because of desire to move quickly, may:

△ Overlook interpersonal factors

△ Close off valuable input from others

△ Stall projects by unintentionally offending others

△ Neglect important details.

Spirited

Because of desire for quickly changing, new input, may:

◇ Become easily distracted

◇ Let spontaneous discussions eclipse tasks at hand

◇ Find it difficult to complete tasks

◇ Find it difficult to organize workspace.

Systematic

Because of desire to do the job right, may:

☐ Become bogged down by detail

☐ Lose sight of the goal

☐ Take too long to make decisions

☐ Miss signs of personal discomfort that could stall a project

Considerate

Because of desire to take care of others' needs, may:

○ Lose sight of immediate tasks

○ Not leave enough time to complete own work

○ Feel uncomfortable pushing through projects for fear of offending others

○ Take on too much and feel overwhelmed.

CHART 3: Time Style Trouble Spots

Capitalizing on Your Time Style

Here are some suggested tips for managing your time in personal, one-on-one, and group situations. There are many ways you can improve your time management. Those presented here are just some samples to get you thinking about how you can better manage that most precious of commodities — your time. Review the suggestions for your style, then go on to the "Action Planning" section on page 13. There you will find thought-provoking questions for making the most of your personal time style.

Tips for the Direct

If anyone will get to the finish line first, it's you. You keep the goal firmly in mind, and no one can steer you off course. If the details do not appear important, you quickly move past them. If group discussions digress, you'll pull people back on track.

The trick is not to make other people in your path feel steamrolled. Remember that you may actually slow down a project when you push too hard. Other people may set up resistance if they feel pushed or overlooked. And by overlooking details, you may be forced to backtrack.

Don't decide too quickly to bypass the details. Allow time for interpersonal discussion. Make room for some spontaneous give-and-take. Who knows? Maybe those brainstorming sessions will actually produce some faster ways of getting the job done.

Tips for the Spirited

If a project becomes bogged down, you're the person who can spark things to start moving again. By providing a sudden flash of insight, you may send people leapfrogging over all the steps they thought they needed to follow to get the job done. Your spontaneity is engaging and motivating.

But taken too far, your spontaneity can cause problems. Although you could keep that creative give-and-take going all day long, eventually the job needs to get done. Keep the finish line in mind. Otherwise, your task-oriented coworkers may become impatient and close their minds to your input.

Remember that organization does matter. Many spirited people find that loose structure and visual cues work well for them. Try keeping like items in your workspace in different colored bins. You may find it effective to put to-do items on sticky notes. Put them on a board within close view. You can rearrange them as your priorities shift.

Tips for the Systematic

Whereas some people may want to get the job done quickly, you make sure it gets done right. You like to look before you leap to ensure that all available information has been evaluated properly. While some people may digress into personal topics, you steer them back onto the agenda and make sure that every item is addressed thoroughly. You're the consummate quality control expert.

The trick is not to let your concern for detail and procedure close your mind to the big picture or to new ways of accomplishing tasks. People who like to move more quickly may become frustrated with you. And those who thrive on interpersonal relationships may feel put off by your focus on tasks.

Let the unexpected happen. Remember that by always adhering to procedure, you may close off some new and better ways of handling tasks.

Tips for the Considerate

Your diplomatic skills can bind together the most diverse personalities and help them work together effectively. You're good at working behind the scenes to listen to people and attend to their needs. Because you are so attuned to other people, you can easily adapt to their ways of accomplishing work. It's hard to imagine a group that could work well together for very long without at least one member as concerned for the welfare of others as you are.

But take that concern too far, and it may turn into a kind of selflessness that doesn't pay. You may not give yourself enough time to complete your own work. Or you may take on too much and end up feeling overwhelmed.

Allow yourself time for your own work. Do not worry too much about offending others when you need to push through a project. In fact, by taking care of your own work, you may ultimately be providing others with more help than you can imagine.

Interacting With Other Time Styles

Handling work our own way usually feels like the best way. But if we insist on doing things our way when we are working with someone whose style is different than ours, friction may arise. That friction can slow work down. Therefore, to be as productive as possible, we need to make adjustments in our own behavior to accommodate the other person's style.

To identify another person's style, observe their behavior. Note the degree of assertiveness or expressiveness used. Highly assertive people are fast-moving. If they are Direct, they like to "cut to the chase." If they are Spirited, they enjoy rapid give-and-take with others.

Highly expressive people don't hold their feelings back, nor do they rein in their use of time. Spirited people always seem to find time to talk to others and entertain them. Considerate people lavish their time on others' needs.

Less expressive people discipline their emotions and their use of time. Direct people channel all their energy into reaching their goals. Systematic people discipline themselves to allow sufficient time to be thorough and accurate.

Recognizing another's time style is the first step in learning to work with others to complete tasks. Although we cannot completely change our own style, we can modify our behavior to make others with different styles feel more comfortable and increase their ability to perform efficiently.

The chart below provides suggestions for interacting more effectively with other styles.

Direct

Behaviors to practice when interacting with the Direct style:

- Make decisions and act quickly; "Cut to the chase"
- Focus on their goals and objectives
- Speak at a relatively fast pace

Friction may arise when Direct people believe you are wasting their time on:

- Procedural details
- Personal topics
- Discussions to weigh all the options
- Brainstorming sessions

Spirited

Behaviors to practice when interacting with the Spirited style:

- Allow time for spontaneous interaction and exchanges of personal information or entertaining stories
- Speak at a relatively fast pace
- Budget in plenty of time to consider various options

Friction may arise when Spirited people believe you are "killing" their spontaneity by:

- Always sticking to a plan or schedule
- Getting bogged down in the details
- Closing out options prematurely

Systematic

Behaviors to practice when interacting with the Systematic style:

- Move through the agenda sequentially
- Allow time for analysis
- Devote discussion time to facts, not opinions

Friction may arise when Systematic people believe you are hurrying things too quickly:

- Not allowing sufficient time to be thorough and analytical
- Deviating from a sound plan
- Making hasty decisions based on emotion

Considerate

Behaviors to practice when interacting with the Considerate style:

- Maintain a relaxed pace
- Allow them time to build trust in you
- Budget in time for everyone to provide input

Friction may arise when Considerate people believe you are ignoring interpersonal issues by:

- Jumping immediately to the business at hand
- Not allowing time to hear everyone out
- Make quick, unilateral decisions

Applying What You've Learned

What's My Time Style? should have given you some insight into how you manage your time in personal, one-on-one, and group situations. This insight will be most useful if you think about how effective your time management is now and how you can improve it by highlighting your strengths and controlling your trouble spots. The following questions will help you to think about your time style and make plans to improve it.

1. What are the positive aspects of your time style?

2. What are some specific ways in which these positive aspects have benefited you in managing your time at work?

3. What are some specific ways that your time style hinders the effectiveness of your time management? Note whether those hindrances tend to involve personal, one-on-one, or group situations.

4. What specific actions can you take to improve how you manage your time?

   Personal

   One-on-One

   Group

5. Can you think of someone with whom you find it particularly difficult to work because that person has a different time style than yours? What can you do to work more effectively with this person?

6. Does your group or team have individuals with a variety of time styles? What can you do to ensure that your time style benefits group activities?

References

Bolton, R. and Bolton, D.G. *Social Style/Management Style: Developing Productive Work Relationships*. NY: American Management Association, 1984.

Jung, C.G. *Psychological Types*. (R.F.C. Hull, Rev., H.G. Baynes, Trans.). Princeton, NJ: Princeton University Press, 1971.

McGee-Cooper, A. with Trammell, D. *Time Management For Unmanageable People: The Guilt-Free Way to Organize, Energize, and Maximize Your Life*. NY: Bantam Books, 1994.

Winwood, R I. *Time Management: An Introduction to the Franklin System*. Salt Lake City, UT: Franklin International Institute, 1990.

For additional copies of this publication, contact the HRDQ Client Solutions Team at:

Phone: 800.633.4533   Fax: 800.633.3683
        610.279.2002   610.279.0524

Online: www.HRDQ.com

ISBN: 978-1-58854-214-4

Publisher: Martin Delahoussaye

Printed in the United States of America on recycled paper.

HRDQ and the HRDQ logo are registered trademarks of Organization Design and Development, Inc.

EN-02-SP-16

About This Product

Developer
Mary Blitzer Field, MA

About HRDQ

HRDQ is a trusted developer of soft-skills learning solutions that help to improve the performance of individuals, teams, and organizations. We offer a wide range of resources and services, from ready-to-train assessments and hands-on games, to facilitator certification, custom development, and more.

Our primary audience includes corporate trainers, human resource professionals, educational institutions, and independent consultants who look to us for research-based solutions to develop key skills such as leadership, communication, coaching, and team building.

At HRDQ, we believe an experiential approach is the best catalyst for adult learning. Our unique Experiential Learning Model has been the core of what we do for more than 30 years. Combining the best of organizational learning theory and proven facilitation methods with an appreciation for adult learning styles, our philosophy initiates and inspires lasting change.